ANTIDOTES TO RICHES IN POVERTY

Make $100 in a week with this (ANTIDOTES)

AYORINDE TIMOTHY

COPYRIGHT

2022 AYORINDE TIMOTHY AYODEJI

ISBN 9798353035206

DEDICATION

This book is dedicated to God Almighty for
his divine mercy and support.

Table of Contents

LINKING OF PAYONEER ACCOUNT TO KDP ACCOUNT

Chapter fourteen

HOW TO MARKET, SELL AND PROMOTE BOOKS.

Chapter one

What's WRITTING?

Writing is that the ability to produce letters or number surface especially using pen or a pencil. Writing is additionally the power to create or to produce something in written form so people can read, perform or use it.

To write clearly, it is essential to understand the basic system of a language. In English this includes knowledge of grammar, punctuation and sentence structure. Vocabulary is also necessary, as is correct spelling and formatting. A writer may write for personal enjoyment or use, or for an audience of one person or more. The audience may be known (targeted) or unknown. Taking notes for study purposes is an example of writing for one's self. Blogging publicly is an example of writing for an unknown audience. A letter to a friend is an example of writing for a targeted audience. As with speaking, it is important to consider your audience when writing. There are many different styles of writing, from informal to formal.

Writing equips us with communication and thinking skills. Writing expresses who we are as people. Writing makes our thinking and learning visible and permanent. Writing helps our ability to clarify our ideas to ourselves.

Types of writing

1.Narrative: This requires you to tell a scene or an event you witnessed in the past. It is when we write a story or give information of the past. In one word, narrative writing is writing about the past.

2. Descriptive: This requires you to give details of a particular thing. Descriptive writing is writing something you know about. You can't write on something you have not seen. Descriptive writing deals with giving details on an object or animal.

3. Expository: Expository essay is much more similar to descriptive essay. In descriptive essay, you describe while in expository essay, you go a bit further by explaining how it's been made etc. For such writing, you need to be familiar with the process involve.

4.Argumentative: This requires you to write for or to write against the topic given. In argumentative writing, the writer is expected to convince the reader.

Chapter two

STRONG WRITTING AND PURPOSEFUL WRITING

Strong writing means no dull moments. It does not imply you've got to put in writing an action-packed story, but it means things must happen in every chapter which will keep your reader reading. Strong writing ensures that the book:

1. Is very interesting, full of anticipation and keeps the reader glancing for more.

2. Has the proper use of words, reasonable and identifiable.

3. Can use and keep readers' attention even when writing about common or simple thing.

4. Fulfills both the desires of the writer and that of the enormous audience

5. Convinces the needs and desire of the audience to the point that they are ready to pay for it at all costs.

Purposeful writing: Purposeful writing could be a specific kind of essay which identifies the author's ideas and evaluates them supported current theory and research. it is written like when the sender talks to the receiver presently.

CLARITY OF GOAL the author has to start with. Your writing should be intentional or purposeful! Your writing must be targeted at accomplishing specific goals. One of the things you must also learn is that you cannot force yourself to write if you are going to have a kind of writing that would be compelling - that kind of writing that carries life and is full of strength! Don't be a failing writer!

Chapter three
BEST SELLERS

Best sellers are books who are sold in thousand copies. For your book to be widely read and sold in thousands copies it means it's a trade book or best seller book.. Some they'll not be written on them as trade book/ best seller book but seeing the thousands of copies sold, it shows that they're bestsellers.

Why does it want to be named a best-seller? The final consensus is that if you wish to create your way onto a best-seller list, any best-seller list, you have got to sell a minimum of 5,000 books during a week, or even 10,000

Chapter four

INTRODUCTION TO E-BOOK

Anything that is read on a computer or handheld device is called an e-book. e-book is also the ability to produce letters or numbers but the difference between it and normal writing is that e-book isn't written with pen or pencil. E-book is an online book or electronic book. From this list we can say e-book is a printed book that can be read on computer or handheld devices. How e-books are circulated E-books are usually circulated on the net as downloadable files which can be read offline, as live web content that has got to be read online, or as sites that are cached by an online browser for reading offline.

Do you want to find out a way to publish an eBook In 2020 alone, eBook sales generated over 1.1 billion dollars! That statistic alone proves why eBook publishing this year can be a requirement for any author. Amazon is now accountable for 85% of eBook sales worldwide. this suggests as an author, if you are ready to publish, you want to search out out the thanks to self-publish with Amazon. With Amazon self-publishing, you'll reach the world's largest book audience and earn up to 70% royalty on your eBooks

Chapter five

MICROSOFT WORD

Why Microsoft word? (WPS, Google doc etc.) Microsoft Word is a word document/app where you type whatever work you have put into writing. Microsoft Word is the document editor that you can take with you on the go. Write and create documents on your mobile device much like you do on your PC There are other word processing apps, like WPS, Pages from Apple, Google Docs etc. But Amazon KDP, works well with Microsoft Word Related to different word processors, it has helpful tools in Spelling & grammar checker, word you'll (It also counts words and lines) Speech recognition Places images in manuscripts Selection of typefaces Unique codes Web pages, charts, etc. Diagrams Shows synonyms of words and can read out the book

How to convert your bok to e-book on Microsoft

. Cover page

• Copyright page

- Dedication

- Acknowledgements

- Table of contents

- Introduction

. Chapters • About the author Copyright© page According to Wikipedia, Copyright its owner the exclusive right to copy, distribute, adapt, display, and perform a creative work, usually for a limited time. The creative work may be in a literary, artistic, educational, or musical form. Copyright is intended to protect the original expression of an idea in the form of a creative work, but not the idea itself. A copyright is subject to limitations based on public interest considerations, such as the fair use doctrine in the United States. Copyright abuse is a crime. It can cost you money and your freedom – imprisonment.

Dedication Page:

This is where the author mentions the names of people his book is dedicated to.

Acknowledgement Page: The author expresses gratitude to the people that participated to the production of the book.

Table of Contents

This is a list of chapters and the page numbers where they begin.

Introduction:

This gives you a summary of the book, who the subject matter are, so that you have an idea before you start reading the book

You should only conclude the introduction when you are done with the whole book. So that It gives a perfect picture of all that is in the book. So, don't start your introduction before writing the story.

Chapters:

This is where plot are laid out, your story is told, and your readers read About the author: Summary about the author

Chapter six

Preparing your book with MS word

It's hard to believe that writers use to jot down full novels by hand. It is sensible that some works of literature are too long because they didn't have a digital application program to assist them cut, shape, and excellent their books. Word processors like Microsoft Word have made books smaller, neater and more excellent than ever before. Microsoft Word is that the application we'll be using to avoid wasting our manuscript documents.

We are visiting only target preparing our eBook using MS word.

Firstly download MS word from your Google play store

Go to Layout > Margins > Custom Margins.

Change the setting for multiple pages to Book fold. ... To reserve space on the inside fold for binding, increase the width of the Gutter. You can add many embellishments to your booklet's appearance. ...

Select Ok

Chapter Seven

Introduction TO FORMATING

Formatting is the laying out of a book to a specific standard, either a British standard or America standard depending on the size of the book. It is also the visual style of a document e.g. Fonts, borders etc. format is the layout of your document in a presentable manner.

   Formatting guides you in building your book in preparation for your eBook creation and publishing.

BASIC PRACTICAL STEPS TO FORMATTING A WORD DOCUMENT FOR CONVERSION INTO AN E-BOOK

STEP 1. Set your page and margin. (Trim paper size to 6"×9")

STEP 2. Choose suitable styles and customize same. (Garamond Font style and Font size 11 is acceptable on the Amazon platform)

STEP 3. Format the interiors - Chapters.

 STEP 4. Fix your cover designate: Title.

STEP 5. Do pagination.

 STEP 6. Headers fixation.

STEP 7. Extras: footers.

Step 8. Add images if available - How?

Step 9. Table of Contents (TOC)

Step 10. Proof and conversion from Microsoft Word (MS to PDF.

Chapter eight

Formatting your eBook with a customize template

WHAT IS A TEMPLATE?

Template is a particular laid down pattern widely accepted, that must be followed when publishing either a hard copy or E-Book.

DEFINITIONS OF TEMPLATES.

��a template is a physical object whose shape is used as a guide to make other objects.

�� It is a generic model or pattern from which other objects are based or derived.

�� It is a chosen or fixed pattern, shape, formula or blueprint that serves as a guide for building up other objects.

�� It is an established formula that can be adjusted to suit ones needs.

�� It is the accepted style to follow as a guide when putting your books together.

♦♦A template is a guide that is to be followed to make other things.

♦♦ It is an accepted pattern/layout/model/guide/formula that is followed in replicating or creating things similar to it.

Chapter nine

PUBLISHING PAPERBACK

To create a new Paperback Title

• Select Paperback

There are three forms you will need to fill before creating the paper back. Some aspects are the same as eBook publishing so we will focus on the fields that are different.

The first form is all about your Paperback details

• Adult Content: Indicate whether the book contains inappropriate material for children under 18.

• Fill all other fields the same way as we did for the eBook details

• Save and continue (or Save as Draft if you are not done)

The second form is all about your Paperback Content.

• Print ISBN: All paperbacks require an ISBN (International Standard Book Number). KDP allows you to use your own purchased

 ISBN, or it can assign you a free KDP one which can only be used by

 KDP for distribution to Amazon and its distribution partners.

To get a free one

Click on Assign me a free KDP ISBN

Select Assign ISBN

 Your book will be assigned a free KDP ISBN • Publication Date: Leave blank since you are publishing for the first time

• Print Options: The page count and ink type determine how printing cost is calculated. Ideally you can use the default settings which are based on the most common selections.

Ink and Paper Type can be:

* Black & white interior with cream paper

* Black & white interior with white paper

* Standard color interior with white paper

* Premium color interior with white paper

The type of book you are publishing will determine the option

KDP will suggest

*Trim Size: This refers to your book dimensions as it will be printed

* Bleed Settings: Bleed allows printing at or off the edge of a page,

 it is used to support images and illustrations. Most books use No Bleed

*Paperback cover finish: Covers can be glossy or matte

• Manuscript: Upload a manuscript of your book interior content.

Supported file formats include

* PDF

* DOC

* DOCX

* HTML

* RTF

• Book Cover: Upload a print-ready PDF cover or Launch Cover Creator, which was covered in the previous chapter

• Book Preview: Preview your file to check for formatting and print quality issues. To do this Launch Previewer

• Save and Continue (or save as draft if you are not done).

Chapter ten

Creating of KDP account.

How to Create an account on KDP STEP BY STEP PROCESS☐☐☐

1: Open your browser.

2: Type the link kdp.amazon.com

3: Click on sign up

4: Click create account

5: Then verify your account

6: An OTP will be sent to you

7: Enter it

8: This would take you to a form where you need to fill your details. !!!!!!

9: Where you see postal code, pleases Google your local government code (the place you reside.) and fill it there. 10: Fill the tax verification form.

11: Sign electronically by inputting your full name

12: Submit, you are done. For Nigerian Postal codes, you can Google it...

Note that for bank details, please choose amazon.com not your local bank

Chapter eleven

Creating your cover page, uploading and publishing your eBook

 A book consist of three parts:

1.The Front matters a.Cover Page b.Copyright page c.Dedication Page d.Acknowledgement Page e.Table of Content Page f. Introduction

2.The Interior (chapters)

3.The Back Page a.Blurb, b.About the Author.

WHAT ARE THE FEATURES OF THE FRONT MATTERS?

 we will look at these more closely now

Cover page: That is the first thing you see of a book. For you to have a good book, all the above listed must be there.

Copyright© page: That's the protection ownership rights to the contents of the book. Note: the information written in any book in the copyright pages, tells you the extent to which you can use the contents and who to contact before usage. Copyright abuse is a crime. It can cost you money and your freedom – imprisonment. Some of the books you buy in our streets/ bookshops in Africa are written by foreigners. If you take them out of the country, you could get into trouble because most are pirated copies. The developed countries of the world take this very seriously.

Dedication Page: This is where the author mentions the names of people their book is dedicated to, and why.

Acknowledgement Page: The author uses this section to express gratitude towards the people that contributed to the production of the book.

Table of Contents (TOC): This is a list of chapter headings and the page numbers where they begin. It could also list major sections that it contains.

Introduction: This gives you an overview of the book, what the subject matter is, so that you have a general idea before you go into the book. You should only conclude the introduction when you are done with the whole write up. It gives a complete picture of all that is in the book in a nutshell. So you may start your introduction, have a draft of it, but finish it when you have the complete picture of what you're writing.

2. The Interior

The second part of a book to be published consists of the main content usually divided into chapters.

This is where the plot is laid out, your story is told, and your reader is mesmerized. This is what the whole book is about, and your content should be split up logically so that it's easy to follow and keep track.

This works hand in hand with your table of contents. What

you are writing about will determine whether you need a conclusion, final thoughts or just a good ending to your story. The third part is the back Page The back page consists of.

The Blurb: This has to do with what the book is all about. It is also called 'ABOUT THE BOOK'

ABOUT THE AUTHOR: This is a brief description about the writer(s) of the Book

Chapter twelve

CREATION OF FOREIGN ACCOUNT.

To receive your payment immediately in your account as your books get sold, you will need to have a satisfactory account for this. Read below the steps to take to help yourself of this. Setting up for Payment – Using Payoneer

Opening an account is straightforward and the steps are below

• Go to Payoneer website https://www.payoneer.com/

• Click Register

• Select Individual from the dropdown list

• Select Get paid by international clients or marketplaces

• Click Register

This opens another form where you now enter the following

• First name

• Surname • Email address

• Re-enter email address

• Date of Birth

Chapter thirteen
LINKING OF PAYONEER ACCOUNT
TO KDP ACCOUNT

Once you have set up your USD bank account using Payoneer, you need to link it to your KDP bank info. To get the bank details • Go to Payoneer website https://www.payoneer.com/

• Sign into your account by entering your email and password

• Click on Receive

• Select Global Payment Service

• Under Approved accounts select View details on the USD account

• Click on Copy account details

• Paste in a safe place

To update KDP bank details

• Log into your KDP account, enter the OTP you received

• Click on Getting Paid

• Select Add bank account

• Select United States from the list

• Copy the following from your Payoneer Account and paste in the KDP Bank info

• Country the Account is domiciled in • Account holder name

• Account type (use Checking) Copy your Bank account name

• Copy your Routing number

• Enter Bank name

• Click Add

Chapter fourteen

HOW TO MARKET, SELL AND PROMOTE BOOKS.

As soon as your book is ready, you need to create awareness to make your book known to the public. One way this can be done is by digital marketing.

The inexpensive form of marketing is the one done by you.

• Share links of your books on Amazon with friends and family

• You can paste them in groups, What Sapp statuses and other social media feeds

You have an option to use KDP's paid marketing services

Digital marketers can be recruited for this purpose also Things that can kill sales include

• Poor editing

• Poor formatting

• Poor design

• Wrong publishing

• Poor Contents

These are all things you should avoid during the book creation and publishing process.

ABOUT AUTHOR

AYORINDE TIMOTHY Ayodeji

Ayorinde Timothy is an undergraduate of University of Education Tai Solarin university of eduction Ijebu Ode. He his a lover of God who devotes himself to the work of God.